LiVELY PARADOX

An Authentic Perspective
on Issues of Diversity & Inclusion

BY NICOLE D. PRICE

Lively Paradox:

An Authentic Perspective

on Issues of Diversity and Inclusion

Nicole D. Price

Lively Paradox

Cover imagery: Ashley Gaffney Designs
Lively Paradox by Nicole D. Price – 1st ed.

ISBN-13: 978-1539000051

ISBN-10: 1539000052

To my biggest fan, my dearest Khalid

...a lively paradox - intellectually stimulating, seemingly absurd or self-contradictory statement or proposition that when investigated or explained may prove to be well founded or true.

Contents

Part I – The Climate

Part II – "You"

Chapter 1: Introduction

...a lively paradox - intellectually stimulating, seemingly absurd or self-contradictory statement or proposition that when investigated or explained may prove to be well founded or true.

In 1980 I started kindergarten. I was ecstatic about the possibility that I would never have to eat celery again. You see, celery and carrots with ranch dressing was a common snack at my preschool. I did not like it as a snack then, and I do not like it now. Often people tell me that they can't remember events from their early childhood. Not me. I recall many things from that year. I remember my daddy teaching me to play the bass guitar and showing me around the warehouse where he worked. Getting to go to the warehouse after school and eating snacks from the vending machine made the celery and carrot debacle worth it on most days.

Lively Paradox

I also remember that a man named James Cleveland Owens died that year. James Cleveland Owens – his name reminded me of the preacher Reverend James Cleveland which is probably why I paid attention. Even as a young person, I spent quite a bit of time in church; James Cleveland could preach and sing people under the pews, which were both things I aspired to do one day. Never mind that the misogyny of the day prevented women from even entering the pulpit, let alone preach (you would also need to overlook the fact that I couldn't sing, either). Had it not been for this slight connection, I likely would have missed the James Cleveland Owens story altogether. After all, he was an African American sprinter. Even at 5 years old, I hated running and took very little interest in running anywhere unless someone was aggressively chasing me. But the James Cleveland Owens story did catch my attention. He was a four-time gold medalist at the Berlin Olympics in 1936. For context, in 1936 Adolf

Hitler was leading Nazi Germany through what he called the creation of a "superior race" that did not include Jews but also excluded black and brown people in general. I was curious. How did Mr. Owens do it? After all, it seemed that even upon death no one even knew his real name. The world does not know James Cleveland Owens, but the world does know Jesse Owens. As it turns out, Jesse Owens was born in the rural, southern United States. A common consequence (not good or bad) of growing up in the rural South is having a distinctive accent. When Jesse's family moved to Ohio in his teenage years, his teachers and peers could not decipher J.C., which is short for "James Cleveland," from "Jesse." So even today I could tell the James Cleveland Owens story and few people would know whom I'm speaking of until I said "Jesse Owens."

Why is this important or significant in a book about difference? It is significant because Jesse Owens was the first person in a litany of individuals who taught me what it looks like to reach your goals when you are the different one. He also taught me what it means to change the landscape for others like you so that they don't have the exact same challenges to face in the future. Consequently, I will reference the Jesse Owens story at various points in this book. Many of those references will be related to race because Mr. Owens's story was a story about race. You cannot tell the Jesse Owens story without talking about race because without that specific difference, I'm not sure there would even be a story to tell.

When I mention the word "diversity" to people, I can hear in the conversation that ensues that they are thinking about race and gender. If you've picked up this book you probably already theoretically know that diversity means much more and includes any kind of difference. While I don't personally believe that we have moved beyond race and gender, this is not a book about race and gender. However – in all transparency – if you don't already know, I am Black and I am a woman, and I think I still could only scratch the surface of the race and gender topic, mostly because of all the rich diversity within female and Black demographics in America. For example, if I was charged with trying to explain what it feels like to be a working woman leaving her child at daycare for the first time, I could not do justice to even that narrow topic. That is mostly because I couldn't wait to drop off my son at daycare and get back to work. My son and I liked each other better with a little space. There are many mothers who wouldn't share my experience or sentiment. What if you broadened the definition of "woman" and included groups that tend to be on the fringes? For example, what if I tried to tackle what it feels like to live as a transgender woman, or a woman who has never had, or even wanted, children? I think you likely get the picture. I cannot fully say what it means or feels like to be a woman or Black, even though I am both. There really is just too much rich diversity within what might seem like a generalized group.

Nonetheless, I have found that there are some universal truths whenever a person or group is underrepresented anywhere or for any reason. This *is* a book about that. We have struggled with difference for a long time. As a result, there are some incredible thought leaders on the issues of diversity and inclusion. This book is not meant to replace their work. In fact, I won't even challenge most of what's come before. This book is meant to build on that foundational work. It is meant to open your mind to the possibility that we can, in fact, tackle the persistent problems that rear their heads when we try to get different people living and working together. There are those who think the answer is in seeing ourselves as the same. I think that's true when you can ditch egos and people work as their enlightened selves – perfect circumstances. The issue is, that is not reality. We all have egos and we love to separate ourselves based on difference. In the spirit of embracing that reality, I profess that we can be drastically different and still work together towards common goals.

Reflection

1. What is your earliest memory of difference?

2. Did you notice you were different or that someone else was?

3. Was your experience positive, negative or neutral?

4. Do you think your first experience shapes the way you view difference today?

Chapter 2: Power Structures

Although this book is not about race and gender, I do want you to know that I am fully aware of power structures. Consistently, underrepresented minorities are imprisoned more, live in food deserts, have subpar schools, are the victims of subprime lending practices, are the victims of tainted water supplies, are disproportionately poor, lack appropriate healthcare and are even killed at greater rates. The fact that this book is not focused on these issues is not an indication of my attempting to skirt the issue. Instead, I have decided two things. First, there are really smart people addressing these issues, and, while I can add to the work on the ground, I can't really add more to the discussion. Second, focusing on disproportionality in large part is not my gift. Quite frankly, it is a very vulnerable position to be in to even share this information with the world. I secretly wish that I were able to take on causes like Bryan Stevenson and the Equal Justice Initiative or Father Edward Joseph Flanagan and Boys Town, but it is not my calling. Please don't confuse "not my calling" with "not my concern." I am concerned about many issues that plague our society at large and wherever possible work to eradicate them. And people like Bryan and Father Flanagan? They've got it. My contribution is to understand the unique challenges of anyone who is different and to mine those situations for success stories. Within those stories lie a few themes. This book represents my attempt to share those themes with you.

Now that we have gotten that out of the way, I want you to look at Figure 1. When looking at the list, I want you to think about what is globally true. I don't want you to think about how things are for some small section of the population. I really don't want you to think about how you wish the world were. Again, think about what is globally true and choose which group is more powerful.

Figure 1

SOCIAL POWER STRUCTURES

MARRIED		SINGLE
CHILD		ADULT
GAY	OR	HETEROSEXUAL
POOR		RICH
MALE		FEMALE
URBAN		COUNTRY
GED		COLLEGE DEGREE

*adapted from Dr. Arin Reeves

Regularly, I have the opportunity to ask that question in front of large audiences and have them say aloud which group is more powerful. Without any prompting from me, the chosen list of words is:

Married

Adult

Heterosexual

Rich

Male

Urban

College Degree

Why is this? How could this be? I mean, how could hundreds of people in unison choose the same words? They can because it simply *is*. We don't have to get together and decide who is disadvantaged on a macro scale; it is obvious even if we don't discuss it. The list of choices could go on and on. I could add Black/ White, religious/ atheist, doctor/ nurse, private school/ public school, citizen/ immigrant, English-speaking/ English-As-A-Second language, etc. It is highly likely that it would be easy for groups to answer in the same, uniform way without even thinking about it. It is for this reason that my first invitation is my first one – not the second or third one. I invite you to **acknowledge what is**. It is imperative that we acknowledge what is in our current state so that we can effectively impact it. How can you fix a problem that you have not acknowledged? Worse, how can you fix a problem that you deny? I am adamant that you cannot. According to developmental psychologist Dr. Robert Kegan, transformation occurs when someone has the opportunity to reflect on something about himself that he couldn't see before and, as a result, can begin to change it. Not one moment before.

One issue of denial that could drive me insane if I allowed it is this notion of not "seeing" color. Really? Isn't that the whole idea? If you have sight, you see color. Skin is different colors, hair is different colors and eyes are different colors. If you walked into a room of all redheads, you would notice. We have got to start thinking about the things we repeat. I get it. To say that you don't see color is a way to say that color is not something that you discriminate against. However, if you don't see it, can you care about it? If you don't care about it, can you be empathetic to the fact that some people create entire systems to separate and disenfranchise whole groups based on something as simple as melanin?

Acknowledging what is does not make you a bad person. It does not magically make you liberal or conservative. It does not make you morally right or wrong. It makes you a realist, real about what is true today. People are sometimes afraid that if they subscribe to what is the reality today, it somehow means that they subscribe to it forever. Not true! Acknowledging what is lays the groundwork for being able to effectively bring about positive change instead of burying our heads in the sand and hoping that somehow, without our acknowledgement, situations will improve.

Reflection

1. Are there differences that matter more or less to you?

2. Are there differences you deliberately try not to see?

3. What would it look like if you practiced **acknowledging what is** around you?

4. Where can you start to practice acknowledging what is? The people, their circumstances, and your own conditions?

Chapter 3: Filters or Confirmation Bias

When you think about the people who personally taught you how to be, who come to mind? Who were the men and women who influenced you and crafted your opinions about what is right and wrong? In your formative years maybe it was your parents? If you didn't have parents, was it the foster care environment? Clearly having parents would shape what you see or even consider as morally right or wrong, versus what you'd think about if you were raised in the dynamic, constantly changing world of foster care. Critical to understanding many of the ideas I plan to share in subsequent chapters is that we are on the same page as it relates to filters. We all have a filter or a lens through which we sift information and cull it down to what makes sense for us. No two people have the exact same filter. Take a moment and jot down your list of inputs – who taught you what was socially acceptable?

Lively Paradox

When I think about who taught me how to be, I think of my mother, my dad, my siblings, my grandparents, the people at church, television, magazines, books, my babysitter Mr. Henry taught me a lot, my friends, my enemies, the social norms in the neighborhood, etc. Furthermore, there were things I learned because I grew up in the city that were different from the things I learned when I spent summers with my grandmother in Mississippi. I learned some things about being a woman that were different from what my brothers learned about how to be men. I even came on the planet with a general disposition and personality. This nature and nurture thing is real.

I didn't realize just how much we were born with until I was an adult. Understanding how I am hardwired has been astoundingly influential in my personal development journey. You would not have known that earlier in my life. In fact, I am not sure I paid much attention to personality instruments until I was in my twenties and working on a team that was highly dysfunctional. I worked mostly with technical professionals because at the time I was actively using my chemical engineering degree. It was an incredibly revealing time. The Human Resources (HR) department visited me and offered to conduct what they called a "high performance workshop." This workshop would use an assessment tool to help me as a leader learn to work better with my direct reports, and it would help to build trust on my team. One thing was for sure: I didn't trust several of my team members. I willfully agreed to the help.

At the high performance workshop, HR facilitated several exercises with my team using the Myers-Briggs personality instrument or MBTI. They had several fun activities that helped us to see how each other approached issues like change management, communication, decision-making and conflict. The interesting thing was that for every one of the topic areas except for decision-making, my team was in lockstep and I was the odd person out. For the first time in my life I had a major work-interest epiphany – it wasn't them, it was me! Looking back on my life in engineering school, I should have seen it. After all, there were plenty of times when my peers seemed genuinely interested in the lab or problem-solving process. Genuinely! And me? Well, I was clearly only interested in the problem-solving outcomes. My concern was simply, "Did it work?" That's it. Another time that should have given me a clue that although I like engineering my personality disagreed was during my internships. In my internships and my early days as a manufacturing engineer, I really liked solving problems and learning about how stuff worked, but I never gave any thought to if I *loved* it or not. Even if you look back at pictures of how I dressed versus how my peers dressed, there was a marked difference. My ivory-colored suit stood out for sure.

I thought about a lot after that day of MBTI activities, and I was determined to find myself and the thing that I loved to do. That experience has certainly shaped me. In fact, it catapulted my desire to help the world understand what it means to be successful when you are different. In that assignment, the way I approached problems, change and conflict was drastically different. My entire way of thinking was different than the majority of the other engineers. Consequently, I had to be skilled at navigating landmines. Deciding to do anything else would have hindered my ability to complete projects. It also could have potentially made it tougher for other engineers who shared my visible characteristics of difference. You know, the race and gender thing? I make this point because I was the only Black, female engineer in the role, too. Inevitably people would have incorrectly associated my different way of thinking to the broader gender and racial groups. The problem with making that connection would have been that it wasn't race or gender that caused me to avoid using spreadsheets to plan my grocery trips, it was a less than linear brain. But we tend to associate differences in the way we think with differences that we can see, like age, ability, weight, race, gender, etc.

Now revisit your list of inputs. What is the probability that any other person on the planet has all of the exact same inputs as you? Let's just call it zero. And here's the thing about inputs, as I get older and have more of my own experiences, I begin to make adjustments to these inputs. Here's what I mean: if I tend to agree with my sister, I will pull a few of her values closer to my chest. I will lean on her for advice and may actively solicit her input when I want someone's opinion on a matter. Conversely, if I disagree with my brother, I will tend to reject many of his values and his opinions. If my brother weighs in on a topic, I might be dismissive – if not irritated – once I have decided his approaches aren't valid. In the same regard, news channels I agree with, I watch. News channels I disagree with, I don't watch. In fact, I have a visceral reaction when I do expose myself to news media where the espoused ideas are the polar opposite of my beliefs. So over time I create a decent filter through which I see the world. When I am frustrated, I go back to my filter, the filter that was first created by my inputs (some of which were given to me). However, it is absolutely a filter that I reinforced based on what I think and what I feel resonates better with me. Then, I constantly am sifting data through that filter for validation.

What does this validation look like? Well, if I am frustrated with you, I might read an article that confirms my position on whatever it is I perceive you did to cause that frustration. The confirmation I receive from that article is my first data point toward proving my view is correct and your behavior is frustrating. Later in the week I may ask my mentor about the same frustrating situation I experienced with you. Generally if I respect my mentor's opinion and seek her out, her thoughts will align with mine. Then I'll have my second data point, which I will treat as proof that my view is correct and validly frustrating. If I see something to the contrary I am likely to dismiss it. I'll search for more evidence to confirm my belief that the situation with you is frustrating. As soon as I find something – anything – there you have it, my third data point! Once I get to three data points, my opinions in my mind are no longer opinions; they are facts. It is called confirmation bias.

Confirmation bias is not about me learning how to work more effectively with you in less frustrating ways. No! Confirmation bias is about me proving myself right. If I really wanted to reduce my level of frustration with you, I would be far better off trying to understand what frustrates me instead of going to my network for suggestions or confirmation that I am correct in my assessments of you and your behaviors. Understanding, not confirmation is the way to that path of peace between us.

So while diversity and inclusion sometimes seem like some issue or topic outside ourselves, for each of us it really begins with a major internal focus. To approach the topic well we have to examine our filters, our biases, and our current approaches. Evaluating these filters will allow us to, first, be able to accept that there are valid reasons why others may not see the world as we do. Then, we will eventually come to fully leverage others in our lives to create amazing results. I fully believe that we will be able to craft a global Ubuntu culture. Archbishop Desmond Tutu defines the African concept of Ubuntu this way:

A person with Ubuntu is open and available to others, affirming of others, does not feel threatened that others are able and good, based from a proper self-assurance that comes from knowing that he or she belongs in a greater whole and is diminished when others are humiliated or diminished, when others are tortured or oppressed... One of the sayings in our country is Ubuntu – the essence of being human. Ubuntu speaks particularly about the fact that you can't exist as a human being in isolation. It speaks about our interconnectedness. You can't be human all by yourself, and when you have this quality – Ubuntu – you are known for your generosity.

We think of ourselves far too frequently as just individuals, separated from one another, whereas you are connected and what you do affects the whole

World. When you do well, it spreads
out; it is for the whole of humanity.

Ultimately the goal is for all of us, as authentically as possible, to present ourselves in ways that facilitate the best possible outcomes for the entire world community leaving the least amount of harm in our path.

Susan Scott would call that our emotional wake. A leader and trainer whose work I respect very much, Susan is the owner of the company Fierce, Inc. , where they are committed to improving lives one conversation at a time. While being certified in Susan's work, I learned this concept called the "emotional wake." It is Susan's trademarked term to describe the impact of having power. Emotional wake is a play on a boating analogy. Little boats create little waves or little "wakes" when in the water. Big boats create big wakes. When Susan speaks of emotional wakes, she is talking about the power leaders have on their teams; and why leaders need to be more careful with their words because they have the ability to cause greater trauma simply because of the power they have. The same is true when you are in the majority group, no matter what that majority group is.

Here's a personal example. At one point in my life I commuted 80 miles round-trip each day to work. Where I lived at the time this was not a common practice, so in order to reduce my carbon footprint, save money and increase my commuting enjoyment, I carpooled with my great friend Stacey and another person. To protect the innocent, we will call the other person "Angie." Both Stacey and Angie were overweight; Angie mentioned that she was on a diet. I was young and effortlessly thin at the time. Because we only had one car at the manufacturing plant, our lunch choices were either to indulge in interesting concoctions from the cafeteria or to go eat lunch at an outside restaurant together. We chose the latter. At lunch one day Angie ordered a salad; she put what looked like a full, 8-ounce cup of Ranch salad dressing on it. It was about 850 calories worth of dressing alone. Then she proceeded to add bacon, cheese, croutons and a few bits of veggies. Before I knew it, I said, "Sweetheart, you may as well order a hamburger." Immediately you could cut the tension in the air with a knife. Was I right? Yes. Was I *right*? No! Technically, I was correct. Her salad had just as many calories as a hamburger and just as many veggies, really. That's not the question. The question is: Do I socially have the right to make certain statements when I am in the power position?

You see, Angie was more socially powerful than me in a few areas; she was married and I was not. She was also a more tenured professional and worked at a higher level, but from a weight perspective I was the powerful one. We were in a restaurant and not at work. So in that moment that was all that mattered. I misused my power.

Since that time I have learned that heavy people are actually discriminated against in so many ways. It is not just ill-placed statements that get strewn at them. People assume that heavy people are lazy, irresponsible, stupid, unemployable, and the list could go on. Sometimes, folks aren't even aware that they're doing it. I regularly take implicit association tests created by Harvard. The IAT measures your implicit associations or subtle associations or biases you have for or against differing groups of people. One of the IATs I took was related to "skinny versus fat" people. In taking the assessment, I learned that I have a slight preference towards skinny. I don't know that this surprised me, however. Even though I could think of a lot of reasons why it shouldn't be true on a conscious level. After all, my mama was heavy. Several of my siblings are heavy. My aunts and uncles are heavy. And I can't believe I am saying this, but my best friend is heavy. Side note: Don't you hate it when someone says, "My best friend is [insert adjective here that is some underrepresented class]"? I do!

Armed with this potentially shameful information about myself (I'm biased against my mama), I set out to pay attention and do something about it. I began picking the heaviest person in my classes as my favorite student. That means, he or she would be the one I asked for help, the first person I would speak to and the one I would joke with and talk with at the breaks. I also started choosing the seat next to the heavy person on airplanes when I flew on airlines that had open seating. I avoided looking at the food choices of heavy people when I was out to dinner or any other meal. Why? Because I was not right. It's been several years since the salad situation. Today, I struggle to lose 10 pounds. God forbid I needed to lose 100. How hard would that be? Now I at least have the empathy to consider another person's perspective and possible challenges. Besides, who made any of us the boss of what other people weigh? In fact, at that time in my life when Angie chose a fattening salad, because she had not asked me for my opinion, it wasn't any of my business what she chose to eat for lunch. I was out of my lane. She hadn't invited me to share my opinion and I did not ask permission to share feedback. I simply, recklessly offered it. This point takes me to my next invitation to you: **Keep your criticism to a minimum (to be read "none") when you are in power**. Rich people can't poor-shame. Thin people can't fat-shame. White people can't shame or demean Black or Brown people. Able-bodied people can't shame the other-abled. Adults can't shame children. Assume ownership of the privilege you have whenever it shows up because if I am the underrepresented minority, your words cut like daggers. When you are in power you have to take responsibility for your emotional wake. There is one exception to this rule: If you are asked for your input privately, you may offer it. However, I want you to remember these words - tread lightly.

Reflection

1. Think about a time when you gave your opinion and you thought the other person *overreacted*. What were the circumstances of the incident?

2. What were the differences between you and this person?

3. Could it be that you were wielding power that you didn't know you had?

4. What are some areas where you have power or privilege? Think beyond race, gender and wealth?

5. Take an Implicit Association Test to uncover your implicit associations or biases. Once you have your

results, make a list of things you can do to mitigate the risks associated with your biases.

Chapter 4: Cost of Effectiveness Drain

When you take a look at introducing difference on teams, or even in families, a very predictable pattern emerges. Let's look at this pattern on a personal level first and then revisit how it shows up in our work lives. My whole family is made up of women and men who can burn (urban vernacular for cooking well) in the kitchen. Once one of my brothers married a woman who could not cook very well at all. Generally when someone joins our family they come with a huge vat of potential. We all want to see brother happy and married for a long time. In this case, everyone wants her to "do" well. Over time that potential diminishes, not by leaps and bounds but in small, predictable leaks. The pattern starts with my brother putting added pressure on his new love interest. I'm certain he shared with her the family tradition of cooking all day the night before a holiday or the massive food assembly lines that were required to pull off the banquets my mother hosted at her church. Everyone was expected to be there, not watching – helping. Sharing this information with her likely added pressure. If I were her, I would start to think about what my contribution to the first holiday gathering would be. At that moment, before she has met anyone, my brother's girlfriend has a little pressure from my brother and a little pressure from herself. That is the first leak in potential.

Whenever a new person joins the family, there is a learning curve. We have some uncommon traditions in our family, just like everyone else, so it will take some getting used to. Let's say the new love interest was a good cook as well. We would forgive her other missteps. We would say, "But she can burn though!" and dismiss her other anomalies. However, she can't cook. So it is likely that when she buys a sweet potato pie from a major retail grocer for Thanksgiving dinner, everyone will give her the side-eye. If, on top of that pie, she has other anomalies, it is simply not going to work. This is the second leak. Family members will start to judge her harshly about everything else because of the cooking thing. These judgments will likely happen in private and not directly to her or to my brother.

In the absence of people trying to help her by showing her how to cook or better accepting her as a non-cook, she will not change her behavior. My brother will pick up on the fact that no one is eating his girlfriend's pies, not even him. Armed with this insight, he may mention it to her. If that is the case, she would likely say, "Your mama said she heard those pies were great. She doesn't have an issue." So my brother lets it go and never gives that kind of feedback again. Third leak! Failure to share feedback or advice (in new roles) is the root cause of almost all issues of difference.

We love my sister-in-law (she still can't cook Thanksgiving dinner) so we would never "fire" her, but that is what tends to happen in organizations when difference is introduced on teams. Whenever it doesn't work out we cite some issue with the "other" person, not the system that killed the possibility. It is the fourth leak related to effectiveness.

When you take a look at introducing difference on teams, people start to tell themselves a story and it creates a very similar, predictable pattern. For ease of explanation I will refer to the person with the difference as the "other." Everyone who is hired on our teams comes to our organization with a huge vat of potential as well. In theory we only hire people we expect to deliver. Over time that potential diminishes - not in leaps and bounds but in predictable leaks – the many times we miss the opportunity or simply do not capitalize on the value a person can bring – or was hired to bring – to the organization.

The organizational pattern creates an **effectiveness drain** on the system. First, the recruiting team focuses on finding a diverse (any diversity) candidate to bring that value directly to the team. This can be a resource-intensive pursuit and a great win when the candidate found is also attracted to the organization. With this valuable new asset, the hiring manager feels tremendous pressure to ensure the "other" is successful.

Figure 2

POTENTIAL EFFECTIVENESS

Everyone has huge vats of potential

Then the leaks begin -
• Pressure to make sure "they" feel welcome

• Internal pressure to be better than average or to fit in

At the same time, the "other" also has exceptional amounts of pressure internally and externally to perform well. It is likely that the candidate herself is highly aware of her difference and what those differences could mean in an environment where she is the minority. The pressure now comes from both entities, each expecting that the "other" will perform at levels greater than the average. That's leak number one. This mindset, which is uncharacteristically burdened with pressure already, has the potential to diminish effectiveness.

Whenever you have a new person join a work team, there is a learning curve. That learning curve is greater when you introduce difference. If I am different than the norm, there are some cultural nuances, some social expectations, etc., that I am not aware of and will likely violate. Because of difference, people are even less likely to provide feedback and suggestions for how to be successful in the existing environment. At times when feedback *is* given, it tends to be more about how to assimilate or be like everyone else which diminishes the benefits of having diverse teams. This lack of feedback creates the second leak. **Awkwardness** from unfamiliarity fosters an environment whereby giving and receiving feedback is laborious. In the absence of credible feedback the "other" continues to perform in ways that may not be the most effective in their new environment, further reducing the vat of potential for which they were recruited to the workplace.

In comes leak three, **Avoidance**, which results from feedback either being uncomfortable to give, being given poorly, and / or received poorly. It grows and it develops into a full-blown story – one that rarely gets edited. Leaders and co-workers say things like, "I tried to give her feedback, but it didn't go well." Then they dig in their heels and refuse to give feedback anymore. The recipient, when asked separately, frequently states she's never heard of these issues before. This gap in giving and receiving feedback can likely be traced to subtleties, sarcasm, passive-aggression, or other ways of being everything but honest and kind. Too many times we talk more about people than we do to people Then we are surprised when the needle is not moving.

Unfortunately, the actual effectiveness of the person over time continues to diminish, resulting in the fourth leak – the "other's" actions don't improve and eventually begin to mirror the faulty perceptions held by the leader and co-workers. So now a situation has been formally co-created whereby leaders really don't think the person can do the work, so they resort to a "why bother" default position. The "other" usually disengages, even if they were talented and highly accountable at the start of the working relationship.

Figure 3

Effectiveness Drain

- Awkwardness based on difference
- Lack of feedback
- Actions unchanged
- See! Look what happens when we hire "those" kinds of people

The results? A profoundly unfortunate ending for the "other," a talented individual who often leaves to find a better "fit" elsewhere; and a major loss for the organization on the unrealized potential of their great recruit. Within the organization there is the continuation of a dangerous cycle of co-creation of failure to benefit from diverse hires and inclusion initiatives; and a tragic reinforcement of biases based on missteps, missed opportunities, and lack of insight.

Often in conversations with talent acquisition teams I will hear individuals say, "We will not lower the bar to gain diverse talent." I think that is an interesting assertion. Lower the bar? I cannot count the times I've seen the bar lowered when someone wanted to hire their niece's husband who doesn't have citizenship status or meet any of the basic qualifications for a job. However, when there is a hearing-impaired person applying for a manufacturing engineering job, he has to darn-near walk on water to be considered. He has to meet every basic qualification just like everyone else, but rest assured, his hearing impairment means he likely has to meet – if not beat – every preferred qualification as well. That, my friends, is called "raising the bar" - not lowering it. It has little to do with personal accountability for the nephew-in-law or the engineering applicant with the hearing impairment. Unfortunately, on the ground that's what we make it about.

In many organizations today there are conversations happening about accountability. I want to talk with you about personal accountability as well, but first you need to understand the opposite of personal accountability – learned helplessness. The definition of learned helplessness is when you come to believe that you have no impact or little impact on your circumstances or the outcomes. It happens when a person has been subjected to trials repeatedly and has been unsuccessful at overcoming them.

A great example of learned helplessness can be found with fleas. If you put fleas in a glass, they all jump out. But if you put fleas in a glass and put a lid over that glass, the fleas will bounce their bodies

against the lid until the most natural thing happens -
they realize it hurts and start to jump just below the
lid. Once ALL the fleas are jumping just below the lid,
the lid can be removed and the fleas will NEVER jump
out of the glass. Ever! Consequently, that's not the
most interesting thing about this phenomenon. In
fact, the most amazing thing actually gives me chills.
You see, even the offspring of these fleas will never
jump out of the glass. Why not? Because they have
learned to be helpless. They tried really hard in the
past and experienced failure, so much failure that now
they imagine obstacles that don't actually exist and
lack the confidence to live fully as they were designed,
as incredible jumpers.

People experience learned helplessness, too. In my
life I have learned four distinct principles to curb the effects
of this brutal cycle:

The Four Things

Number 1 – **We all are here on this planet for a unique reason, just as fleas have the capacity to jump.** We each have to believe in our innate ability to do something unique in this world. Sometimes we find that something and other times it finds us. Regardless, I believe that <u>every</u> person has a unique gift or calling.

Number 2 – **Sometimes some person or system will, in essence, place lids or obstacles in our way.** In those moments, we can't be idle. We have to step into the power we have and keep practicing our craft, so we are ready when the opportunity comes. Keep jumping as high as you can. You will need those skills later.

Number 3 – **Those of us with power, privilege, and influence have a responsibility to help remove lids**. We have a responsibility to remove obstacles when we see them. This is especially important when you are in a position of power. It is easy to tout accountability when you are outside the glass. What are you doing to help when you are outside of the glass?

Number 4 – **Open your mind to the possibility that former obstacles do not present challenges today.** Remember you can jump, and don't allow past failures - or worse, the past failures of others - to hold you back. Imaginary lids are the hardest to combat and that's mostly because we have convinced ourselves in our minds that they exist. We are hardly a match for the power of our minds.

If we are going to do anything to impact the persistent challenges that plague us, we have to include a conversation and some action towards removing lids. It is irresponsible to talk about the "other" jumping out of the glass otherwise.

Reflection

1. Have you ever withheld good, proven advice because you didn't want to upset someone?

2. Have you ignored good or proven advice because of who suggested it?

3. The next time you encounter an unfavorable outcome on your team, practice talking to your teammate instead of about her or him.

4. When have you been told someone's story before you even worked with him or her? Think about how it might have affected your experience.

5. Do a "flea jar assessment" of your own life – at work or otherwise. When have you felt too repeatedly defeated to try again?

6. Now, consider when someone you know seemed to lose all motivation? Was there anything you could do to help?

7. Be cognizant of your ability to impact change in the life of another. Sometimes we're the flea, but sometimes we're the lid. We need to recognize both.

Chapter 5: Course Correction

When discussing issues of diversity and inclusion, people often bring up the idea of personal accountability on the part of those who are different. And when we begin conversations about supporting great diversity the focus inaccurately goes to competence, even when a far better conversation – one more attuned to what we know happens from the study of learned helplessness – is that of actual and perceived limitations. First, remove any identified limitations. Second, work to rebuild a more accurate sense of the current reality and restore confidence that new things are now possible. In other words, the first step is to remove the lid – at least remove the lids that are within your influence. Remember, power structures? Acknowledging that they exist is not terrible. Where you have the ability to do something about lids, do. Where the limitations are clear, consciously make time to think about what you can do to help, but also delve into areas where those limitations may not be as obvious or visible.

Because once the lids are removed we have a foundation for truly being inclusive and diverse. If we are working and living with people who are consistently subjected to lids, then we are diminishing the possible contributions they can make. We are contributing to the leaks, either actively or by ignoring them altogether. Consequently, it is not just harmful to them; it is harmful to all of us. We have no idea what could be accomplished if all the ideas were allowed at the table.

This conscious effort is important. Leadership coach Tara Jaye describes it this way: "We all _know_ what we personally experience. We each _value_ what we know. We then behave according to our personal values. Then our brains proceed to _create mental shortcuts_ in the name of efficiency, reinforcing our existing behaviors. Mental shortcuts are the enemy of inclusion because doing anything outside your natural inclination requires intentional thought. And what does intentional thought require? You guessed it – consciousness. We need to uncover ways to increase our consciousness."

Increasing our consciousness is also important because in today's environment most destructive behavior is not egregious. In fact, when it is typically an army of support is deployed to the affected person or group's defense. When a lone, domestic terrorist entered a church on a Wednesday night in Charleston, South Carolina, and killed nine worshipers in the name of hate, the entire United States empathized with the congregation and the mourning family members. People called the assailant "sick" and "disturbed." No one wanted to be publicly associated with this type of hatemongering. The support was vast and wide. Fortunately, in our organizations people are not regularly coming in with handguns and killing.

Unfortunately they are slowly, subtly killing people with their words and indirect deeds every day. It's called micro-aggression.

Micro-aggressions are the everyday verbal, nonverbal, and environmental slights, snubs, or insults, whether intentional or unintentional, which communicate hostile, derogatory, or negative messages to targeted persons based mostly upon their membership to a marginalized group. Micro-aggressions are more damaging because stress is cumulative and support is lacking. Support comes from all around when people are viciously attacked, but when a person or group is the target of many small attacks support is virtually absent. Many times the victims of micro-aggressions are left wondering were they really slighted at all. If they do see a pattern of negative treatment, sometimes the actions are so minute that it is "not worth bringing up" the issue with someone who can help. If the issues are brought up, then the victim is in danger of hearing that he or she is being petty. They may even be asked to be more positive and give the aggressor the benefit of the doubt.   That advice is not entirely wrong. Here's why: Often the aggressor has not given much thought to his or her own behavior, which is worse than deliberate aggressions. At least with deliberate aggressions the person is aware, and awareness is the first step in changing any behavior. George Bernard Shaw said, "The worst sin towards our fellow creatures is not to hate them, but to be indifferent to them; that's the essence of inhumanity."   Increasing our awareness is one way to address indifference.

Where the "benefit of the doubt" and "positivity" messages go wrong is that humans don't just *lose it*. Again, stress is cumulative, and this gradual, repeated maltreatment can create a volatile situation over time. The good news is we can do small things to positively impact situations for the better, if we are operating from a state of consciousness.

The Harvard Implicit Association test is a good way to increase your consciousness for those things you are subconsciously biased towards or against. A subconscious bias is an assumption that we make – a prejudice that we have – that we may not even realize. It's not something we've thought about and consciously decided on. It's not based on reasoning, sound or unsound. Frequently unconscious biases can be seen in some of the associations we make automatically, like: Veteran status to gender, being physically fit to intelligence, having weaponry to race, or many other correlations that, beyond our socialization, have very little to do with each other.

There are some things people are openly biased against. For example, every couple decades a new generation enters the workforce. Whenever this happens the other generations consciously get together and discuss all the things wrong with these "young people today." They openly talk about it. "Young people" seem to be a group that is getting older and older with each passing year. Recently a person was pontificating about issues with "young" people. I inquired about the actual age of the people he was referring to, and he said 35! Thirty-five? Jesus only lived to be 33 years old. So there you have it. Jesus, if alive today, would be classified as "these young people."

Unconscious bias is not so overt. It is sneaky. We have no idea about our subconscious biases. In fact, subconsciously we can be biased against things we ARE. There's a way forward, though. First, I encourage you to find the time to take Harvard's Implicit Association Test (IAT). It is a widely recognized tool for uncovering subconscious biases. I have mentioned the IAT before, but I strongly encourage you to take as many of the assessments as your time permits. Once you are aware of your implicit associations you can work to correct your behavior, but not one moment before. I mean, do you really think I was purposefully taking a seat on an airplane next to a person whose body might spill over into my seat before taking an IAT revealing my bias against heavy people? I was not. I was mostly oblivious to the subtle and not-to-subtle aggressions towards heavy people. Had I not taken a seat next to a heavy person on several flights, I would not know just how mean-spirited people can be regarding this issue. I've heard people say, "He should buy an extra seat." I have heard them say, aloud, "That's a shame to get that big." Well, maybe he should buy an extra seat. I don't know. But what I *do* know is that those statements were mean. Robert Brault said it best, "Today I bent the truth to be kind, and I have no regret, for I am far surer of what is kind than I am of what is true."

Lively Paradox

This issue of bringing people together is not likely to occur within group conversations. It probably won't occur with passive-aggressive comments on an airplane either. It can only occur if I open my mind to my issues first, my biases and implicit associations. Even before I do that, I know one thing for sure: **You can be honest and kind.** In addition, wisdom is knowing *when* to share information, even if it is the truth.

There was a dress code at my first engineering job. There still is – khaki pants and a polo-style shirt. It was my least favorite thing to wear. So I didn't wear it. Because this dress code was the unwritten kind, technically there was no way for me to know it existed. One year at performance review time, instead of discussing the millions of dollars I saved the business my manager Dave was talking about my lunch choices and my clothes. Today I laugh about it, but then I was furious! You see, I used to go to the plant dressed exactly the way I dress today – in colorful skirts. In my mind, the only things I needed to worry about were that I had on safety glasses, steel-toed shoes and a hard hat (it was powder blue). Imagine me in my Pepto Bismol™ colored skirt, a flowy blouse and safety gear, standing on top of a printing press. I wish I had a picture. What I know today is that Dave was trying to have a conversation with me about credibility. People expect certain roles to be dressed a certain way. Imagine for a moment that your lawyer came to court dressed like your gardener, or vice versa. You would wonder about credibility. The problem is, Dave didn't just say that. He tiptoed around the dress issue like it was the plague, and I would get so frustrated because we weren't talking about the work. The truth is that the work wasn't getting in the way – my lack of khakis was. Now before I lose you, people should be able to wear whatever they want. They can't though. You want to know why? Because those of us who understand that the clothes don't always make the man (or woman) won't do what's necessary in the short-term to impact these conversations more broadly in the long-term.

I respect Dave, but he was allowing political correctness to get in the way. It's inevitable when you don't trust yourself. If Dave had done some self-work to know where his biases were, he could have shown up more authentically. If I could go back in history and help Dave out, the conversation would have gone like this: "Nicole, I am a bit nervous to talk with you about something because I am afraid you will think this is about you having a different style. That is not what I want. I want you to know that this conversation is about you being rewarded and promoted for your darn good engineering work. The respected engineers around here wear khakis and polo shirts or some version of that outfit. People here find it to be more credible. You may wear what you want; I just want you to know that when you walk in a room right now people are more concerned about your clothes than they are your proposals. I support you either way. I just thought it would be helpful to you to know how perceptions work around here."

I could have made my own choices based on his feedback, but as my leader he owed me the input. Wearing a lapel pin doesn't make a president any more or less patriotic until he or she doesn't wear the appropriate one. At that moment an ounce of metal becomes the most important thing in the world, regardless if it is or not.

Once I have some understanding of my own issues, I can practice **micro-affirmations**. I created the acronym ALIVE to help you recall the ways in which you can personally affirm someone you are struggling to work with or for a group of people you've identified that you are subconsciously biased against. I am confident that this list can also help you with your conscious biases as well.

A is for Awareness You have to first be aware of your propensity to be biased in order to care enough to do anything about it. You also have to stop arguing about the impact of things you consider to be inconsequential. You don't get to determine how someone else is offended. Affirm!

L is for "Let It Go." Release all preconceived ideas and remove any judgment you have about the other person or situation. Check ego at the door and rise above any personal motives, swapping them out for behaviors that benefit the greater good of the organization. Here are some specific ways you can do this:

1. Understand that while you might have grown up with, be married to, or otherwise be familiar with a group of people, each individual is his or her own person and may not fit traditional stereotypes.

2. When you have strong opinions (favorable or unfavorable), evaluate whether those opinions are facts or "facts" you created based on your filters.

3. Remember that if everyone had the same strengths and weaknesses we would also have all the same blind spots. Give people the benefit of the doubt.

I is for Involvement. Seek out ways to interact on a personal level with others or in the worlds' of other people. Invite them to participate and keep everyone in the loop. Be socially inclusive. Listen to different music, try other foods, go experience something that would be new to you but is commonplace for someone else. It helps to improve your worldview and your relationships. But know that relationships improve on a one-on-one basis by getting to know people on a personal level. Avoid trying to improve relationships with people by taking on issues of difference in public. Relationships do not improve in public forums; understanding happens in more intimate settings. You can accomplish involvement in tactical ways:

1. Get to know people as individuals first in private, one-on-one conversations.

2. Remember that no one person can speak for the whole of any group.

3. Do not make assumptions about what you think other people will or won't like to do. Ask.

V is for Virtuous. Be honest. Be honorable. Be upright and give credit where it's due. Encourage others' strengths and acknowledge their accomplishments. Be transparent about what you don't know and be open to feedback. Also, virtuosity means sharing the unwritten rules of the organization where possible.

Whenever you are the other, you need sponsors. These are people who will support you when you aren't in the room. They will also share great feedback with you to help you navigate any landmines. I worked for an organization once where the CEO questioned the motives of anyone who backed into a parking spot. For him it represented a person who couldn't wait to leave work at the end of the day, which suggested in his mind a lack of commitment. I grew up in a precarious neighborhood. Backing your car in was a safety measure. It allowed you to get out fast in an emergency and also helped you to see if someone was following you home. It had nothing to do with commitment to anything except survival. My credibility with the senior leadership could have been reduced solely on the merit of something as simple and arbitrary as parking style. What if someone hadn't shared this unwritten rule with me? Never mind the merits of his approach or mine. The purpose of me sharing this is to help you see the importance of transparency. Here are three methods for demonstrating transparency:

1. Once you understand your biases (conscious or subconscious) it is dishonorable to act as if you do not know. Create a plan for examination.

2. Speak up for others when it matters, in their absence.

3. Share information regarding the secret codes in your organization or family.

Finally, E is for Examination. Examine yourself. Take a look at the simple things you could do. Simple things like making a point to say "hello" and "goodbye" matter. In general be friendly, and take it to another level by asking others for their input. Pay attention to when you purposely avoid looking at others and dig in to see what that's about. Did you know that avoiding eye contact is a way to create separation? There's a study that suggests looking another person directly in the eyes for four minutes results in feelings of admiration and even love. Don't believe me? Notice how you look away from your spouse or love interest when you are angry. Better yet, notice the way people tend to look away from a salesperson when they want to walk away from the deal. To bring people together, make eye contact.

Listen. Try not to interrupt others when they are talking. Many of us are spending so much time trying to be understood that we fail to take time to understand. Here are some points of examination:

1. Critically think about why you might not notice certain people or groups or hear their concerns. Are your reasons credible?

2. When you won't do the small things, ask yourself why. For example if you feel like, "I don't have to say hello." Really? It's such a simple thing. Why not?

These small gestures will help you create a foundation of good, solid relationships so that diversity and inclusion efforts will have staying power in your organization. Good relationships require that you address your biases and any micro-aggressions that create a difficult work climate for the people you interact with most closely every day. When we are displaying inclusive behaviors we are helping, not hindering or judging, and building people up instead of draining them. This is certainly a very kind thing to do.

Reflection

1. Find some time to take 2 or 3 of Harvard's Implicit Associations tests.

2. Once you have your results, practice consciously working against one of your personal biases.

3. Can you think of a person or persons who sometime get under your skin? What is the source of your pain? What are you thinking about this person?

4. Instead of judgment, try offering up a micro-affirmation to them the next time you see them.

Chapter 6: Who Cares?

The phrase "business case for diversity" is used in an attempt to move beyond mere legal compliance with EEO and affirmative action laws. The theory is that in today's global economy there is value in the diversity of thought and perspective that employees from a wide range of cultures and backgrounds can bring to a business. Organizations that employ a more diverse workforce should be able to deal more successfully with their increasingly diverse customers. More diverse companies, then, should achieve better business results – higher sales and profits and a stronger corporate reputation.

In the not-so-distant past, the first step in business was to understand what the business case for diversity meant. The next step was to understand what it meant for all businesses, and the final step was to understand what it meant uniquely for your business.

Benefits of diversity were touted to include:

- Easier recruiting and access to a wider employee base because the company becomes an employer of choice

- Increased engagement among a more diverse employee base, leading to higher productivity

- Better decision-making and creativity because more perspectives are brought to a problem

- Improved employee retention

- Improved corporate and brand reputation which is achieved by appealing to the growing diversity in your consumer base, potentially giving you an advantage in product development and marketing, and ultimately in sales and market share

- Obtaining a more global perspective on your business, leading to better supply chain sourcing and lower costs and/or higher quality

Those are all well and good, but the truth is **diversity hurts.** Let's face it, things are easier if everyone thinks, acts, marries, dines and worships just like me. Do you recall what this looks like on the ground? Remember that when a new person with difference comes into an organization, she comes with added pressure. The pressure comes from two sources. First, the hiring manager has increased pressure to make sure that the new employee is successful. Second, the new and different employee has some pressure to make things work with her new peers. Both parties realize that there might be some challenges. However, the unknown usually manifests privately. We don't typically have open conversations about the challenges. If you think back to my Jesse Owens story, there was pressure from his coach and from himself to be successful. If Jesse Owens failed, it could have damaged or setback inclusion efforts in track and field for years. The coach was likely thinking about his reputation in the sports community. Now let's look at Jesse. He wasn't the only African-American racing on the Olympic team, but he was the one the world was looking at. What if he failed? What would that mean for track and field on the Olympic level? What would that mean for race relations around the globe? This pressure diminishes potential. Walk through the other system leaks that were discussed in Chapter 4. The result is the deduction that "we should not hire these kinds of people anymore." Sometimes this is overt and other times it is subconscious. The system will push out the difference. Then, the vat of potential winds up empty. The different person either completely disengages or leaves, and the organization ends up with more of the same. We don't know how good we could be at times because we don't muscle through the tough stages.

Because of changing demographics, more demanding customers, and mobility across borders, organizations were told that they needed to shift how they attracted, retained, and developed talent. They were told that they also needed to create a more inclusive environment that leveraged diversity effectively. While I am a fan of doing things because I feel they are morally right, business decisions are made because they are profitable or will lead to profits.

So what's the issue? Well, in the very city where I lived for most of my life, a major employer is not focused on any of these things. When other companies in the area are participating in supplier diversity efforts, they are absent. You also don't see them at any events that are specifically related to diversity. Guess what though? It doesn't seem to matter. Financially they are doing better than many other organizations in the city. They are growing like gangbusters. Additionally, consider Silicon Valley: It is one of the most homogeneous business districts in the country. Yet, the innovation coming out of the Valley is unmatched. Why? Is the issue that diversity doesn't matter? I think not. The issue is that diversity is hard, man! We introduce difference and act like it's all going to be smooth sailing. It's not. Diversity invites another level of judgment, and judgment is the number one thing that hinders innovation. Innovation is your natural state when you aren't judging.

I was at a retreat in southern California, and one of the evening activities uncovered the connection between innovation and its inverse relationship to judgment. At dinner that evening, with spectacular food and perfect weather, we were invited to have robust conversations with each other. But we couldn't say any of the things I just said. We could not describe conversations as robust or stale. We were to avoid describing the food as scrumptious or disgusting. The weather? It was neither perfect nor awful. We could not use adjectives to describe anything. Adjectives were deemed to be simply judgments, and we were to have a judgment-free meal. We were invited to talk about anything else we wanted, just so long as it was not subjective. After all, who decides if a conversation is robust or "too deep?" Serve up chicken to a vegan and all of a sudden even Popeye's fried chicken is a pile of dead muscle on a plate. That day in California it was a sunny, breezy 72 degrees Fahrenheit and getting cooler as dinner went on. I have a friend from Brazil who would have certainly preferred the temperature to be about 10 degrees warmer, so even using the word "perfect" to describe Southern California evenings was a judgment.

We did it. At first there was mostly silence, but after a while we did start having judgment-free conversations. In that judgment-free zone, we affirmed each other; we came up with options to persistent issues; we were innovative. They were right, innovation is your natural state when you aren't judging.

Here's another, more personal example: My best friend is a preacher. Once at her church they decided to wear wristbands to remind them not to gossip about or judge other people. During our very first phone conversation after that service, she and I were silent. We had nothing to say. It was a shame, really. We had become so used to talking poorly about those other people out there who just didn't see the world like us, that we had nothing to actually talk about when commanded to stop talking about people. Soon we were able to have discussions. Then we started discussing ideas. It felt like we solved many of the world's problems when we stopped talking about people. Again, when you introduce difference, you introduce judgment. We talk more *about* people than we do *to* people and think that somehow our relationships will improve. Our solution, even if it is not overt or conscious, is to surround ourselves with like-minded people. Judgments are decreased and innovation thrives. My question to you is: What could we accomplish if we were able to introduce difference and eliminate judgment?

When asked when there would be enough women on the Supreme Court, the "Notorious RBG" - better known as Justice Ruth Bader Ginsberg - nonchalantly answered, "When there are nine." If that bothers you, then you should certainly be bothered with the numbers as they have been for hundreds of years. If it is not okay to have all female justices, then how could it be okay to have all male justices? Diversity is the difference that shows up as the "butts in the seats," but inclusion is actually leveraging all the talent that diversity brings. In recent years people have started to say that they are not counting butts in seats. Stop counting butts in seats and nothing will change. Well, it will be the turn of the century before we see, gender numbers that represent the make-up of our populations.

When organizations are diverse and inclusive and judgment is at a minimum, research still shows that those companies outperform companies that aren't taking active steps to be diverse and inclusive. I may be creating innovative product and making a ton of money doing it, but what is the difference between being successful and making a significant difference? What is the impact of improving life for a small percentage of the world versus improving life consistently for a larger group of people? Maybe it is about you? Maybe it is about something much larger? Using profit as the only measure is shortsighted. What about people from a global perspective? And let me tell you what I know for sure: Profit and people don't matter one bit if the planet is not a consideration.

So, is it impossible to have difference on teams and in our families and live without judgment? Clearly it is hard work. We will never feel like doing it. But to say that it is impossible is a fallacy.

"Impossible is just a word thrown around by small men who find it easier to live in the world they've been given than to explore the power they have to change it. Impossible is not a fact. It's an opinion.

Impossible is potential. Impossible is temporary. Impossible is nothing."– Muhammad Ali

Reflection

1. Try creating a judgment-free environment around you. Did it make the innovation flow freely?

2. Were people more comfortable with sharing ideas, no matter how wild they seemed?

3. When was the last time you had a conversation with a like-minded person that didn't involve talking about folks who were different from you?

4. When you get ready to judge, think of ways you could help instead.

PART II: You

Chapter 7:   Transitioning to YOU

When I think about what it takes to be successful in a diverse working environment when you are the different one, there are some specific strategies that come to mind. However, I absolutely abhor when people conflate issues. So let's be clear, there are lids. I am in no way saying that the system doesn't need to be addressed.   I am not suggesting that people practice patience in the meantime.   After all, it is hard to be patient when there's a foot on your neck.   What I am saying is that there are short-term solutions and long-term solutions, and we must consider both. I also don't want you to think that I am asking you to jump out of a glass with a lid on it.   That would be ridiculous. Although I know that sometimes in life people will hold lids on glasses and then tell you stories about the one little flea they knew who jumped onto the lid, held on upside down with its little flea hands, crawled along the underside of the lid, and then squeezed its way out to freedom. I am not intending to tell you stories like that. In fact, recently in the media there were these amazing stories of two high school students who managed to become valedictorians of their high school classes while they were homeless. I think that's awesome. I can't imagine the obstacles they had to overcome in order to make that happen. It is an indication of the power of the human spirit. With that, I want you to contrast those two children with the number of children who are homeless in America: 2,500,000. Clearly, we need to work to get food and shelter for children, and not expect superhero powers.

In the next chapters, I am going to share with you the consistent themes necessary when you are different, underrepresented, or on the fringes of societal norms. I will share how you can lead your life; how to jump as high as you can while the lid is on. These themes are not being shared in exception to lids being removed. These themes are being shared in conjunction with lids being removed. One is not at the expense of another.

Today if I were shot by a police officer, the conversation in the news media would ultimately arrive at the question of why don't people in the black community concern themselves with black-on-black crime. Look, I respect the badge. Several members of my family put their lives on the line every day to keep their communities safe. I appreciate that they do it. Let's be clear, I would not. At the same time, if I am unlawfully shot and killed by a police officer, that has nothing to do with whether or not there is black-on-black crime. In fact, the term should be banned because every murder victim is likely to be killed by someone of the same race. With that, since we don't use the terms "white-on-white" crime or "Hispanic-on-Hispanic" crime, we should not use black-on-black crime. It isn't a real thing. Furthermore, if I am killed unlawfully, police should be the first to come to my defense as enforcers of the law.

As I share these themes, keep these examples in mind. I know that I am conflating issues into one book. I need you to know that I am not conflating them in my mind. They are different. This second section is for you. It is not for you to assimilate. It is not for you to lie down and take it. It is designed for you to impact what you can on the micro level or in the short-term, so that ultimately there is a shift or a tipping point on the macro level or in the long-term. This is not about patience. This is about power. It is designed to help you move fully into the power you do have so that you can lead your life.

Chapter 8: Confidence

A little known Black History fact is that a man named Eddie Tolan won two gold medals in track and field in the 1932 Olympics. Eddie was known for chewing gum while he ran and needed glasses to see, so in 1932 that meant he taped them on to keep them in place during races. Why is this significant? It is significant because prior to 1932 there were no Blacks competing in the Olympics. Why not? Did Blacks suddenly become competent to run at that level? Of course not! It is not a competence issue. Never mind Jesse Owens for now. We have established that he did great work. What you may not know is that he wasn't alone in 1936 Berlin. There were 18 Black American athletes competing in those races. Jesse is the one we all remember because of his 4 medals. Eighteen is not a huge number. It also is not one. Imagine being Tolan and being the only one. It had to be terrifying.

Thank goodness courage is not the absence of fear; courage is deciding to take an action even when you are scared out of your mind. Eddie Tolan did not need competence. He needed confidence. It was the confidence that he could do it that allowed him to pave the way for Owens and everyone after him.

If you want to lead your life well, you cannot expect that someone else will build your confidence. Sometimes, in the words of Kind David, you have to encourage yourself. There are some specific ways to do that.

Think about your goals

Keep your goals in front of you. Remember them. You can use a vision board or something similar to remind you what you want. When I went to engineering school, the administration asked each of us to create a fake degree. They told us to make sure it looked like the real thing, had an accurate date, and included anything else we thought would be helpful (letter of honors for example). In manufacturing environments this approach towards keeping your goals in sight is called visual management. These kinds of visuals are helpful. Never expect that someone else will do this for you. They might, but don't expect it.

Be open to support from unconventional sources

Be careful not to have too many rules about who can inspire you. If you don't have an actual mentor, what keeps you from reading the exceptional advice from an inspirational figure? I am a huge fan of Nelson Mandela. Clearly I cannot meet him as he has transitioned. However, if I want advice about how to bring groups in conflict together for a larger goal, I read his memoirs. I still follow him on social media.

If someone wants to help you, allow him or her to do so. If it is not illegal or unethical, help is help. Would you receive assistance from someone who you disagree with politically? What about someone who is always late? Would you be open to their strategies for being timely? Most people would say no. But I challenge you to reconsider that. Just because I have not mastered something doesn't mean I can't offer good advice. Some of the best experts I know in the field of leadership development are not the best leaders themselves, and we all listen to their advice.

Create short-term mile markers

Your goal may be a stretch goal. In fact, those are awesome goals. Create smaller steps that are necessary to reach the larger goal. Track your progress on your smaller goals. Celebrate in some tangible way every time you reach a smaller mile marker. Also, don't forget to remember where you started. Sure, sometimes there are down moments. But usually your down moments are still higher than where you started.

Find role models

Find someone somewhere who has accomplished something similar to what you are trying to do. I regularly use this exercise with adults in my leadership classes. The details aren't important; what is important is that adults never accomplish the mission on the first try. I bet they wouldn't accomplish it even with an unlimited number of tries, if I didn't tell them that small children could do it on the first attempt. In this case the only difference between the children's and adults' performance is belief. The children believe it is possible where the adults typically think the mission is doomed from the start. So, I found inspiration for my leadership groups in an unconventional place –

with children. My point is for you to find your example wherever you can.

Be careful of conventional wisdom

This advice may seem counterintuitive after I just mentioned finding examples, but don't be bogged down by this notion that you need a role model. Oprah Winfrey did not have a model to follow for what she is doing today. It did not exist for women, it did not exist for poor children, and it did not exist for Black people. There was no model of a multibillion-dollar media powerhouse who started where she did. Oprah is an example of the power of imagination. You don't always have to be a realist.

Helen Keller is my favorite example of seeing what could be and dreaming of a better reality without being able to actually visualize it - literally. Helen could not see or hear. In 1904 she was the first deaf-blind person to earn a Bachelor of Arts degree. That feat was considered impossible before Helen did it. Today, it is an expectation that deaf, blind, and deaf-blind children get an education. Helen did the really hard work with her instructor on a micro level. She helped to change the game for students with special needs. Things on the macro level changed because Keller did the work. She dreamed of something that did not exist.

Understand that the issue is not competence. Fleas can jump. The issue, typically, is confidence.

Reflection

1. When was the last time you imagined? I mean, no holds barred, flat out, full on, dreamed? What was that dream?

2. Find some time to visualize. Write a letter to yourself from the future or, if it's not too cryptic, write what you want to be said of you at your funeral.

3. Consider creating a vision board; if collage isn't really your speed, take it to Pinterest or simply write your goals down.

Chapter 9: Commitment and "Rise" Factor

Even if you have all the confidence in the world, there will be setbacks. You will run into obstacles. That is a fact of life even if you are part of a majority group. It is certainly true if you have elements of difference. But do you know how hard it is to bounce back in the face of obstacles, if you aren't committed to your goals?

Have you ever wondered why judges, civil servants and many professionals take an oath of office? Why they insist on goal setting and signing a commitment statement in Weight Watchers? One could argue that it is about legalities; that we sign agreements and contracts in order to have documents to refer to. However, did you know that saying "yes" to someone else – out loud, while looking him or her in the eye, increases your chances of actually following through on your commitment? What does this have to do with you and leading your life? You have to commit to doing your part.

I have a friend who works in a highly artistic, very small business. This business has been operating for more than a decade but it is still a young company. The employees lack the structure of large corporate engines and so does the owner. Consequently, my friend is the different one. She grew up working in some powerhouse businesses and has a pulse for how operations scale-up. Every day she is frustrated. When we are on friend calls I simply listen, but every once in a while she'll request a coaching call. The coaching calls are funny. She says things like "I don't care about these incompetent people." The interesting thing is that she is right about their incompetence. But she's not doing her part, either. She is their leader. Leaders develop people. Each coaching call we end up right back there; if the people don't have the skill, get it to them.

Humans like to pontificate about how people should be. Then when they show up differently, instead of us demonstrating what we would like to see and adjusting a little, we have the temerity to insist that everyone adjust around us. Ludicrous! I invite you to identify what you *do* have the ability to influence. Often when people are all up in arms, there are a few things at play. They are not focused on their goals and what they can do right now, today, to move one step closer to those goals (i.e. effectively lead the people). Another possibility is that they are out of their own lane and focused on something that's none of their business. I am guilty of this one. Stay in your lane and be clear about your goals.

It is not always clear whether there are lids or if we are sometimes imagining lids that have been removed. If there's a chance that the lid or obstacle is imagined, then you need strategies for rising up after the fact. One of the best tools I know for questioning thoughts that might be holding you back is from *The Work* by Byron Katie. If you aren't familiar, she offers her "Judge-Your-Neighbor" and "One-Belief-At-A-Time" worksheets for free on her website, thework.com. The purpose of these tools is to help get you to a neutral place versus an emotionally charged place, so that you can do the work necessary to make the leap. The tools are completely about questioning your thoughts. When I was first exposed to The Work, I was in a peculiar place in my life. This is a very personal story, but stick with me because it will explain the power of The Work. I was in my third marriage (please don't judge me harshly), and my husband at the time had dated a woman before me who was a church pastor. I called her "the crazy preacher lady." When he and I started dating, the crazy preacher lady would not go away. She called regularly. Once she even came to my job to let me know just how much he loved her. He said they had broken up years before, but she wasn't done with this relationship at all.

When I showed up at the Byron Katie Cleanse event that she hosts every year on New Year's Eve and New Year's Day, I was off-kilter a bit. The people I saw there were a little weird and upon first blush appeared to be kind of cultish. It was also New Year's Eve, and instead of being with my family I was with my boss in L.A. We were bunking in the same room. I don't really like rooming with others. In fact, I don't particularly like living with others. Did I mention I am the sixth of seven children? I've had my share of sharing space. This trip was also shortly after my mother had passed away, and I was still grieving; I had married my boyfriend, and the crazy preacher lady was on my last nerve. She called him even more now that we had gotten married. But I had recently subscribed to this idea that if you can't get out of something, get into it. So I was going to make the most of the Cleanse.

At the Cleanse the instructions are pretty simple: every time you were frustrated, angry, lonely or hurt, fill out these worksheets. I followed the simple instructions. I had so many worksheets by the end of the first day it was ridiculous – just wasting trees left and right. If Byron Katie said something irritating, I did a worksheet. If my boss invited friends back to the room, I did a worksheet. If I was cold, hot, bored, whatever, I did a worksheet. And of course the crazy preacher lady got her own worksheet – actually several. Nothing was happening, but I kept filling them out. Then on night two, the most amazing thing happened. I woke up from my sleep with this epiphany: The crazy preacher lady's actions were not my business. She was not *my* ex-girlfriend; she was his. It was his business to handle, not mine. All of a sudden it felt odd even to call her crazy. This was not some positive psychology trick either. I fully believed it. I was free. I was so free I wanted the preacher lady to call. Guess what? As soon as I had done the work and released it, she never reached out to me again. It is amazing how the universe will stop teaching you lessons once you learn them.

You might not have a crazy ex. You might not be like Jesse Owens or Eddie Tolan with a whole country of people who hate you. But if you are different you will, or have, run into some obstacles that are taking up too much of your mental energy in the present moment. Reflect on what those things are, and then I invite you to fill out the worksheets. If you are anything like me, your ego might be saying, "I don't need to fill out worksheets. That's stupid!" Don't listen to your ego; it is not very intelligent. Trust me. Your results might not be immediate, but you will find your way to peace. In that peaceful state you will be positioned to rise up.

Reflection

1. Visit www.thework.com and download the Judge-Your-Neighbor worksheet.

2. If there is any area of frustration for you, fill out a worksheet or two and see what you learn.

3. If you learned nothing, take advantage of the free hotline on thework.com and get a little help through the process.

Chapter 10: Circle of "Control"

Okay. We've covered a lot of information so far. I've share statistics and research, historical references, personal examples, tips, tricks, and even worksheets. I'm going to peel back one more layer to be even more transparent with you right now: I'm hesitant about this chapter. My fear is that after all we've been through in these 100-or-so pages that something in this chapter will rub you the wrong way and undo all the work we've done up to this point. I'm taking a chance here.

Have you ever seen the movie *The Untouchables*? Sean Connery and Kevin Costner play detectives determined to bring down a major mafia figure played by Robert De Niro. In it, Sean Connery has this line – this question that he poses to Costner's character whenever he gets overwhelmed because all the odds seem against them: "And what are you prepared to do?" It's a question that brings the focus back to the detectives themselves and the things that are within their control.

Figure 4

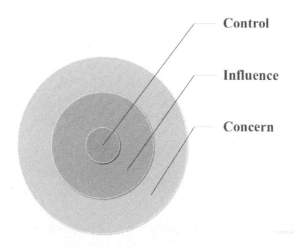

Control

Influence

Concern

What is within your control? There are likely many things that concern you. That's normal. But look at the figure above; your sweet spot is in the middle circle. The fact that you are different, the fact that your team mates may not be accustomed to dealing with difference, the hard reality that by and large our society has been on autopilot for so long that many do not even notice when they are committing

infraction upon infraction based solely on difference –
none of that is within your control. So, what can you
control? Your performance. You can, in the face of
unfavorable odds, continue to be as exceptional as
you've always been. You can continue to grow and
develop and leverage your difference as the asset that
it truly is. In fact, you more than can – you must. This
is personal accountability. What are you prepared to
do?

If you can only be successful in perfect
circumstances, you are in a quandary. Your
circumstances will rarely be perfect. Once I worked
for an organization that can best be described as
"loosey-goosey." Everyone was kind of open-ended,
fly-by-the-seat-of-the-pants types. We had the best
ideas but we rarely executed them flawlessly. We
were in desperate need of a project manager so we
hired one. That's what you do when you are emergent

and just jump right in. Our project manager was perfect. He finished all of his projects. He had back off schedules and Gant charts. He was great. We, on the other hand, drove him crazy. He had to adjust his timelines more times than was reasonable. Sometimes he would even have to fly out to the Midwest to make sure things were in order. He would follow-up in email, voicemail and text, just to get the simplest things done. He could have given up. He could have been frustrated. Weird thing is, he never let it show. Consequently, I found myself wanting to help him. He changed me not by pointing out how irresponsible we were but by being flexible and easy to work with.

You have to choose to perform in spite of the obstacles, and trust, there will be plenty. But you have to decide to succeed anyway. One thing that may help you stay focused is remembering the three Ps: purpose, passion, and prowess.

It is likely that your purpose comes so easily that it doesn't even occur to you that it's something others cannot do. It's the thing that people always call you about; the thing that you make time for, even when you're super busy. Have you considered that *that* is the thing you could be doing with your whole life? Purpose will pick you back up when a bad day knocks you on your butt because the work you're doing? It's bigger than you.

Passion is what happens when you're not resistant to your purpose. The work you'd do for free? Passion. That subject you continue to study, even though you've been done with school for years? Passion. It is what will help you keep going when others would get tired. For me, I have found my passion in work. However, I am more passionate about the arts. So I could be as tired as ever, but if I get invited to see a play, to hear my favorite band or to go to a comedy show, all of a sudden I have energy that I thought was depleted. Wholeheartedness is the antidote to fatigue. You are more likely to be wholehearted about something you are passionate about.

What about prowess? What are your skills? It's not always enough to know your purpose and be passionate about it. If your purpose and passion do not overlap with your prowess, you obviously have work to do to address that learning curve. But it can be especially hard to put forth the effort if you are "good" at something already. It can be a challenge, as Jim Collins puts it, to make that leap from good to great. However, it's a worthwhile and necessary leap because we've already discussed that different plus average just doesn't fly. It is estimated that you need to put in 10,000 hours to be great at something. Do the work. Be the best you in your field, whatever it is.

But let's be clear: The lids are real. Remember that flea story? You can jump all you want, you can even fly, but if the lid is on – you're going nowhere. If you can acknowledge that and hurl your whole self into it anyway, something will have to give. A breakthrough is inevitable. Don't get so used to looking up and seeing a lid that you stop looking up altogether. You might recall that the enemy of personal accountability is learned helplessness. Work on you, be ready when opportunity knocks on your door. Jessie Owens practiced. He was ready so that when he got his chance at the big race, he could effectively compete. Don't be that flea who decides it's not worth jumping.

That being said, if you live a comfy life outside of that glass, you have things you can influence as well. One of those things is to help impact the narrative. Maybe children can be valedictorians and be homeless at the same time, but you may not make your exceptional flea a token. If you are outside the glass and have a warm place to sleep every night, don't turn a blind eye to the homeless. You may not use a single, extraordinary success as an excuse for not providing resources, coaching, and opportunities to others. The goal is to work to create the exceptions while also working to change the rules.

Reflection

1. What are your three Ps? Do they intersect or overlap?

2. In what area of your professional life have you been "good enough"?

3. What comes natural to you? Is there room to strengthen that skill?

Chapter 11: You Are Right! Now What?

You are different and people don't treat you the same. I don't personally need you to convince me of that. In fact, I would be surprised if you were different and people did treat you the same. It is a rarity, really. So you are right, but how effective are you? How happy are you? Take the reigns and do everything within your power to get the results you want and find happiness.

Let's look at it from another perspective. Many times when we are open to the viewpoint of someone who is vastly different, it is generally because they are exceptionally gifted in some other area. For example, if someone is really rigid about schedules and timelines and we aren't so much, we will put up with it if that is so helpful to us that we couldn't get a project completed without their support and regular guidance. When someone is vastly different from us and yet the relationship works, two things are present: we are open and they are valuable. It is a rare occasion when someone has average (or worse, subpar) work habits, produces marginal results, AND he also falls outside of what is broadly defined as "normal."

Take for example, the effort we will or won't put into learning people's names. I am fascinated by unique names, and I find it interesting when people say they cannot pronounce unorthodox names. Really? We know how to pronounce Condoleeza Rice, Andre' Igudala, Ben Rothlisburger, Mark Zuckerburg, and any other name of someone who has proven to be exceptional. Which means we have the ability to pronounce names we find difficult, but we generally only put forth the effort in exceptional cases. People we find to be average we give nicknames, usually without their permission. I'm not saying it's right.

For now, it just is. And it is a good example of the minor ways in which my next point is true – **if you are unorthodox you must also be exceptional.**

One of the reasons I left my job in corporate America to work for an entrepreneur was because I liked the rapid-fire nature of the work. I enjoyed the curve balls that consulting on this level brought. At the time, the opportunity was to travel the country speaking and teaching. In order to do that work, you have to live a life that is flexible, nimble, open-ended and pressure-prompted. All of those characteristics are generally not combined with scheduled, step-by-step, methodical and early starting. With that in mind, our collective team had some skill gaps until we added someone with those skills to the team. This addition actually helped us plan better and get our projects completed under budget and on time. But here's the other part of the equation: When you are the different one, diversity should not hurt. It cannot come at a high price or be emotionally expensive.

You can't hold your uniqueness over other people's heads, making them adjust to you all the time and stopping the action instead of figuring out how to move the action forward. Our new team member couldn't show up touting all the projects we couldn't do because they didn't fit into his Gantt chart. No! He listened to all the outlandish things we'd propose for the calendar, and instead of saying "No!" he found hundreds of ways to say, "Yes." He would take our list, go talk with stakeholders, put things in a calendar with a back-off schedule, and then let us know what targets we had to meet in order to reach our goals. If he'd showed up at the meetings talking about how this or that was impossible, we would have been about ready to kill him. Well, maybe not kill him, but the system would have fired him – pushed him out. People would judge his behaviors right or wrong, tattle, sabotage, and work to preserve the system of sameness that worked for them. Even if it really ain't working.

It helps to find ways to invoke your point of view that are not off-putting to people. This is not about assimilation or becoming just like everyone else. We lose twice if we encourage people to assimilate – they suffer, and, worse, we don't get the value of their differing perspective. I mean, who wants to assimilate, coming to work every day, acting like someone they're not? It isn't about changing who you are or being inauthentic; it is about using what you are to benefit, not create pain or cost. That would be a sure fire way to increase disengagement, and this is about being effective. If you are different you cannot afford to be ineffective, and trust me, you also cannot afford to be average. Our newest team member is exceptionally gifted in his ability to get things done. It's simple math, he benefits the team more than he costs the team. For this reason, not only do I allow him to manage my projects I allow him to manage me – to a point.

Reflection

1. What are you better at than anyone else you know?

2. What makes you exceptional?

3. Do you have a team member who's a whiz at one thing or another? Is that person different in a very obvious or recognizable way?

4. Conversely, do you know a colleague who is, by all accounts, average? Does this person fit the criteria for "normal"?

Chapter 12: Pedagogy of the Oppressed

There was an experiment involving five gorillas in a cage. Every day a bunch of bananas was placed on top of a ladder in the cage. The gorillas naturally wanted the bananas. However, as soon as one gorilla would attempt to get the bananas, all five gorillas would be sprayed with cold water. This process was repeated whenever any gorilla tried to retrieve the bananas, and eventually all the gorillas stopped trying.

Once the gorillas started to consistently avoid the ladder and the bananas, the scientists replaced one of the five gorillas. As soon as the new gorilla saw the bananas, of course it attempted to climb the ladder. But this time instead of being sprayed with cold water, the other gorillas attacked him and prevented him from getting to the bananas. They assumed they would get sprayed with water and didn't want that to happen, so they made sure the new gorilla avoided the bananas. After a couple of failed attempts the new gorilla learned to leave those bananas alone if he didn't want to be attacked.

The scientists then replaced yet another gorilla. The second replacement behaved the same way the first gorilla did, and it too was attacked. Amazingly, even the first new gorilla that knew nothing about the spraying took enthusiastic part in the attacks.

The process of substitution was repeated until all five original gorillas had been replaced with new ones – ones that had never been sprayed with cold water. Each time a new gorilla attempted to get the bananas, the other gorillas would stop it.

This practice is prevalent with gender and board service and C-suite assignments. Women in senior roles, especially if they were only ones when first promoted, are notorious for being harder on other women. They avoid seeking out women to help and are offended at times with requests to lead gender parity efforts. They take on the characteristics of men. Paulo Friere shared this phenomenon with us in his book *The Pedagogy of the Oppressed*. None of the gorillas in the cage knew why they shouldn't be climbing the ladder, yet none of them would try again nor would they allow the others to do so. One reason for their behavior was that it's just the way things had always been done. Another reason is that we take on the characteristics of our oppressors when we don't spend time thinking critically about our approaches and our statements.

I recall when I was choosing the brand colors for Lively Paradox. Against the advice of the designer, I opened the decision-making up to several friends and colleagues. I was thinking that whole "use the knowledge of the tribe" thing. At any rate, several women came back to me and said that the palette was feminine. I had two questions. First, what makes leadership not feminine? Second, aren't I a woman? What good is being different if I completely lose the thing that brings a different perspective?

I met Sarah Thomas in 2016, shortly after she was named a referee in the National Football League. Sarah told me about the rigorous nature of the approval process. She also informed me that the process was highly data-driven. No one makes it to referee status at the NFL level without being competent. However, I had a question for Sarah surrounding what specifically being a female added to the game on Sunday mornings. Now given that she is equally as qualified (that's already been established), I wanted to know what she added to the game from a female lens. She proceeded to tell me that when a young running back gets a concussion she's more concerned. Her mother instincts take over. She's making decisions as if he's her child and not just another player on the field. Now could a man do that? Absolutely! Is it more likely that a woman would? Highly likely.

Getting to the next level of leadership, infiltrating a new family unit, invoking creativity in the technical arena, being the first Native American female on the Supreme Court – what do these things matter if you lose the unique lens through which you see the world? That's the beauty of diversity. That you bring forth the expertise you have in a way that provides something the larger group would have missed. If you lose that, we may as well have stayed homogeneous.

Reflection

1. Have you ever minimized your difference?

2. What do you wish people in power knew about your perspective and experience?

3. What are some things you want to remain true to once you reach certain goals you've outlined for yourself?

Chapter 13: Start Where You Are

Part of the reason some of our diversity efforts aren't sticking is because we can't get people to buy-in to doing the work necessary to get to positions of influence and actually affect change. Another thing that happens is that by the time a person of difference gets to a position of influence, she has lost so much of who she was that she starts to preserve the original system that she was intended to help change or improve. Both things are important – adjust to gain credibility and then remember that it was an adjustment. Once you have arrived at a level of influence, or if you are at a level of influence, do not turn a blind eye to the lids. Help to take them off. Help to create environments that get the best use of all the talent you have available to you. If you aren't there yet, I invite you to consider what you can do to get there. Remember, your circumstances are not the reasons why you can't reach your goals. If you landed in a precarious situation, you can get out of it. How do I know? You wouldn't be here otherwise.

Oprah Winfrey recounts a story about the first time she listened to one particular preacher at a seminar in 1969. She was an A-to-B student and thought she already understood the importance of doing her best. But that day, she says, this reverend lit a fire in her that changed the way she sees life even to this day. His speech was about the personal sacrifices that had been made for all of the Black students in that audience, regardless of the horrible history and brutality of the Transatlantic Slave Trade. The preacher talked about those who had come before her and her classmates, the people who'd paved the way for them to be sitting in an integrated high school in Nashville, Tennessee, in the late 60's in America. He told them that what they owed themselves was excellence. "Excellence is the best deterrent to racism," he said, "Therefore, be excellent." She took him at his word. That evening Oprah went home, found some construction paper, and made a poster bearing the preacher's challenge. She taped that poster to her mirror, where it stayed through her college years. Over time she's added her own adages: "If you want to be successful, be excellent." "If you want the best the world has to offer, offer the world your best."

"The best deterrent to racism is excellence. Therefore, be excellent." Diversity and inclusion is about far more than race and gender, and I think that quote applies to any kind of unfair treatment. Today Oprah Winfrey is one of the most powerful women in the world. I believe you have it within your power to envision the world you want for yourself and live solidly in that purpose – excellently. In the words of the late tennis player Arthur Ashe:

Lively Paradox

"Start where you are. Use what you have. Do

what you can."

Reflection

1. Whose story inspires you? What can you take from their experiences and apply to your own life?

2. Write down a mantra that moves you, and put it somewhere you can see it every day.

3. From this day forward, try accommodation instead of critique. Think, how are we alike? What goals are we trying to reach that we agree on? Start there.

Sources

Curious about any of the people, events, theories, or studies I mentioned in this book? Feel free to dig deeper. They're listed here by order of appearance in the book.

- James Cleveland Owens, 1936 Olympics
- Bryan Stevenson, Equal Justice Initiative
- Father Edward Joseph Flanagan, Boys Town
- Dr. Arin Reeves , *The Next IQ*
- Archbishop Desmond Tutu, Ubuntu
- Muhammad Ali on "Impossibility"
- Dr. Ian A. Roberts, *Prisoners or Presidents*
- Susan Scott, *Fierce Conversations*
- Harvard, Implicit Association Test
- Robert Brault on "Kindness"
- Flea Study, 1910. *"On the behavior of spiders and insects other than ants"* by C.H. Turner
  https://www.youtube.com/watch?v=1733vephnZo
- Tara Jaye Centeio, *Say Yes*
- Charleston Nine
- Eddie Tolan, 1932 Olympics
- Helen Keller, *The Story of My Life*
- Byron Katie, *The Work*
- Gorilla Study, 1967.*"Cultural acquisition of a specific learned response among rhesus monkeys"* by G.R. Stephenson
  https://www.youtube.com/watch?v=VbBeqrRZF9Y

- Paulo Friere, *Pedagogy of the Oppressed*
- Oprah Winfrey, *What Oprah Knows for Sure About Doing Your Best*
- R. Roosevelt Thomas, *Beyond Race and Gender*

Attending a Lively Paradox Session?

If you are attending a session (or already have live or virtually), prior to engaging in the training, please review a few items in order to get the most out of the experience.

The intended outcomes are to uncover individual biases, level-set the knowledge base and to have a set of shared experiences for reflection beforehand and to help with the creation of your development plan. This content will provide context for discussions and guide the commitments you decide to make after the session as well.

Required

1. **Implicit** - Take 1-2 of the implicit biases tests created by Harvard University. **Note: You will need to click "I wish to proceed" first. Then select whichever tests you want to take. The descriptions are listed. Each assessment takes less than 5 minutes.
   https://implicit.harvard.edu/implicit/takeatest.html

2. Watch General Welsh – **Leading Your People** (10 minutes)
   https://www.youtube.com/watch?v=Kb_oFqVqdms

3. Watch Chimamanda Ngozi Adichie – **The Danger of a Single Story** (19 minutes)
   https://www.youtube.com/watch?v=D9Ihs241zeg

Reflection Questions from Pre-work

1. What were the exclusionary practices and what biases showed up during General Welsh's speech?

2. What "ah-has" did you have, if any, from the other material?

3. What information builds on what you already know?

About the Author

"Nicole was AMAZING!"

"You have to attend this!"

"[It was] the best leadership/management training I've ever attended."

These are just a few of the responses from seminars and training courses based on the Nicole D. Price Lively Paradox model. If leadership is anything, it's personal, and she gets this. It is possible to effectively lead a team with many different personalities. And she'll teach you how.

Nicole holds a Bachelor of Science degree in chemical engineering from North Carolina A&T State University and a Master of Education degree in adult education from Park University. She is certified in many of the leading assessment tools and, as part of her practice, works with some of the best and brightest in leadership development. Nicole has led enterprise-wide leadership development efforts within a Fortune 500 company, and she has consulted with hundreds of organizations on leadership, accountability, change management, and diversity & inclusion.

Every team member brings individual qualities and quirks, but difference doesn't have to be debilitating. In fact, it can be inspiring. Nicole believes that with the right strategies you can have a high-performing team where everyone's hard work pays off, professionally and personally.

To learn more about Lively Paradox, our services, or to book Nicole for speaking, training, or development opportunities, please visit: www.livelyparadox.com/booking

Be Connected

Visit our website
Go to www.livelyparadox.com to learn about new webcasts or white papers, to read exclusive previews and excerpts of new books or to book us for keynotes. You may also reach us by filling out a contact form at http://www.livelyparadox.com/contact-1/

Follow us on Social Media
@livelyparadox

Get quantity discounts
Books are available for a discounted rate when you purchase 20 or more, or when you book a speaking engagement.

Made in the USA
Monee, IL
16 March 2022

92943610R00083